50 Global Noodle Recipes

By: Kelly Johnson

Table of Contents

- Pad Thai
- Spaghetti Aglio e Olio
- Ramen with Pork Belly
- Pho with Beef Brisket
- Soba Noodles with Sesame Sauce
- Fettuccine Alfredo
- Pesto Pasta
- Udon Noodle Soup
- Singapore Noodles
- Bún Thịt Nướng (Vietnamese Grilled Pork Noodles)
- Japchae (Korean Stir-Fried Noodles)
- Egg Noodles with Chicken
- Laksa (Spicy Noodle Soup)
- Noodle Kugel
- Italian Pasta Salad
- Dan Dan Noodles
- Macaroni and Cheese
- Khao Soi (Thai Coconut Curry Noodles)
- Carbonara
- Cold Soba Noodle Salad
- Yakisoba (Japanese Stir-Fried Noodles)
- Spicy Thai Noodles
- Baked Ziti
- Lo Mein
- Mie Goreng (Indonesian Fried Noodles)
- Aglio e Olio Spaghetti
- Tantanmen (Japanese Spicy Noodles)
- Chicken Noodle Soup
- Jajangmyeon (Korean Black Bean Noodles)
- Hakka Noodles
- Bihun Goreng (Fried Rice Vermicelli)
- Vermicelli Salad
- Noodles with Garlic and Oil
- Beef Stroganoff Noodles
- Thai Peanut Noodles
- Italian Gnocchi

- Shanghai Noodles with Pork
- Shrimp Scampi Pasta
- Miso Ramen
- Khichdi (Indian Rice and Noodle Dish)
- Noodle Salad with Vegetables
- Hungarian Noodles with Cabbage
- Zucchini Noodles with Marinara
- Curry Noodles
- Fideo (Spanish Noodle Dish)
- Spicy Sichuan Noodles
- Noodle Bowl with Tofu and Veggies
- Bun Rieu (Vietnamese Crab Noodle Soup)
- Soba Noodles with Dipping Sauce
- Pancit (Filipino Stir-Fried Noodles)

Pad Thai

Ingredients:

- 8 oz rice noodles
- 2 tbsp vegetable oil
- 2 garlic cloves, minced
- 1 cup cooked shrimp or chicken
- 2 eggs, beaten
- 1 cup bean sprouts
- 3 green onions, chopped
- 1/4 cup crushed peanuts
- 3 tbsp fish sauce
- 2 tbsp tamarind paste
- 1 tbsp sugar
- Lime wedges (for serving)

Instructions:

1. Cook rice noodles according to package instructions.
2. Heat oil in a large pan, sauté garlic, and add shrimp or chicken.
3. Push to one side, add beaten eggs, and scramble.
4. Add cooked noodles, fish sauce, tamarind paste, and sugar. Toss to combine.
5. Stir in bean sprouts and green onions. Serve with crushed peanuts and lime wedges.

Spaghetti Aglio e Olio

Ingredients:

- 12 oz spaghetti
- 1/2 cup olive oil
- 4 garlic cloves, sliced
- 1/4 tsp red pepper flakes
- Salt to taste
- Fresh parsley, chopped (for garnish)
- Grated Parmesan cheese (optional)

Instructions:

1. Cook spaghetti according to package instructions.
2. In a pan, heat olive oil, sauté garlic until golden, then add red pepper flakes.
3. Drain spaghetti, reserving some pasta water.
4. Toss spaghetti in the pan with garlic oil, adding pasta water as needed.
5. Season with salt and garnish with parsley and Parmesan.

Ramen with Pork Belly

Ingredients:

- 4 cups chicken broth
- 2 packs instant ramen noodles
- 1 cup cooked pork belly, sliced
- 2 soft-boiled eggs
- 1 cup bok choy
- 2 green onions, chopped
- Soy sauce (to taste)
- Chili oil (optional)

Instructions:

1. In a pot, heat chicken broth.
2. Add ramen noodles and cook until tender.
3. Stir in bok choy and cook for another 2 minutes.
4. Serve in bowls topped with pork belly, soft-boiled eggs, green onions, soy sauce, and chili oil if desired.

Pho with Beef Brisket

Ingredients:

- 4 cups beef broth
- 1 pack rice noodles
- 1 lb beef brisket, cooked and sliced
- 1 onion, sliced
- Fresh herbs (basil, cilantro)
- Bean sprouts
- Lime wedges
- Hoisin and Sriracha sauce (for serving)

Instructions:

1. Heat beef broth in a pot.
2. Cook rice noodles according to package instructions.
3. In bowls, layer noodles, brisket, and onion.
4. Pour hot broth over, then garnish with herbs, bean sprouts, and lime.
5. Serve with hoisin and Sriracha on the side.

Soba Noodles with Sesame Sauce

Ingredients:

- 8 oz soba noodles
- 1/4 cup soy sauce
- 2 tbsp sesame oil
- 1 tbsp rice vinegar
- 1 tbsp sugar
- 1 tsp garlic, minced
- 1 cup sliced cucumber
- Sesame seeds (for garnish)

Instructions:

1. Cook soba noodles according to package instructions.
2. In a bowl, whisk together soy sauce, sesame oil, rice vinegar, sugar, and garlic.
3. Toss cooked noodles with the sauce and cucumber.
4. Garnish with sesame seeds before serving.

Fettuccine Alfredo

Ingredients:

- 12 oz fettuccine
- 1/2 cup butter
- 1 cup heavy cream
- 1 1/2 cups grated Parmesan cheese
- Salt and pepper to taste
- Fresh parsley, chopped (for garnish)

Instructions:

1. Cook fettuccine according to package instructions.
2. In a pan, melt butter, then add heavy cream.
3. Stir in Parmesan cheese until melted.
4. Toss pasta in the sauce, season with salt and pepper, and garnish with parsley.

Pesto Pasta

Ingredients:

- 12 oz pasta (e.g., penne or fusilli)
- 1/2 cup pesto
- 1/2 cup cherry tomatoes, halved
- 1/4 cup grated Parmesan cheese
- Salt and pepper to taste

Instructions:

1. Cook pasta according to package instructions.
2. Drain and toss with pesto, cherry tomatoes, salt, and pepper.
3. Serve topped with Parmesan cheese.

Udon Noodle Soup

Ingredients:

- 4 cups vegetable broth
- 8 oz udon noodles
- 1 cup sliced mushrooms
- 1 cup bok choy
- 2 green onions, sliced
- Soy sauce (to taste)

Instructions:

1. Heat vegetable broth in a pot.
2. Add udon noodles and cook according to package instructions.
3. Stir in mushrooms and bok choy, cooking until tender.
4. Serve in bowls, seasoning with soy sauce and garnishing with green onions.

Singapore Noodles

Ingredients:

- 8 oz rice vermicelli noodles
- 2 tbsp vegetable oil
- 1 onion, sliced
- 1 bell pepper, sliced
- 1 cup shrimp, peeled and deveined
- 1 cup bean sprouts
- 2 garlic cloves, minced
- 2 tbsp curry powder
- 3 tbsp soy sauce
- Green onions, chopped (for garnish)

Instructions:

1. Cook rice vermicelli noodles according to package instructions, then drain.
2. Heat oil in a large skillet, sauté onion and bell pepper until softened.
3. Add shrimp and garlic, cooking until shrimp turns pink.
4. Stir in curry powder, soy sauce, and bean sprouts. Add noodles and toss to combine.
5. Garnish with green onions before serving.

Bún Thịt Nướng (Vietnamese Grilled Pork Noodles)

Ingredients:

- 8 oz rice vermicelli noodles
- 1 lb pork loin, marinated and grilled
- 1 cup lettuce, shredded
- 1/2 cup cucumber, sliced
- 1/2 cup pickled carrots and daikon
- Fresh herbs (mint, cilantro)
- Crushed peanuts (for garnish)
- Nuoc cham (Vietnamese dipping sauce)

Instructions:

1. Cook rice vermicelli noodles according to package instructions, then drain.
2. Slice grilled pork into thin strips.
3. In bowls, layer noodles, lettuce, cucumber, pickled vegetables, and pork.
4. Top with fresh herbs and crushed peanuts. Serve with nuoc cham.

Japchae (Korean Stir-Fried Noodles)

Ingredients:

- 8 oz sweet potato noodles (dangmyeon)
- 2 tbsp vegetable oil
- 1 onion, sliced
- 1 carrot, julienned
- 1 bell pepper, sliced
- 2 cups spinach
- 2 garlic cloves, minced
- 3 tbsp soy sauce
- 1 tbsp sesame oil
- Sesame seeds (for garnish)

Instructions:

1. Cook sweet potato noodles according to package instructions, then drain.
2. Heat oil in a pan, sauté onion, carrot, and bell pepper until tender.
3. Add garlic and spinach, cooking until wilted.
4. Stir in noodles, soy sauce, and sesame oil, tossing to combine.
5. Garnish with sesame seeds before serving.

Egg Noodles with Chicken

Ingredients:

- 12 oz egg noodles
- 2 tbsp olive oil
- 1 lb chicken breast, diced
- 1 onion, chopped
- 2 garlic cloves, minced
- 1 cup broccoli florets
- 1/4 cup chicken broth
- Salt and pepper to taste

Instructions:

1. Cook egg noodles according to package instructions.
2. In a large skillet, heat olive oil, sauté chicken until cooked through.
3. Add onion and garlic, cooking until softened.
4. Stir in broccoli and chicken broth, simmering until broccoli is tender.
5. Toss in cooked noodles and season with salt and pepper.

Laksa (Spicy Noodle Soup)

Ingredients:

- 8 oz rice noodles
- 2 tbsp curry paste
- 1 can coconut milk
- 4 cups chicken broth
- 1 cup cooked chicken, shredded
- 1 cup bean sprouts
- Fresh cilantro (for garnish)
- Lime wedges (for serving)

Instructions:

1. Cook rice noodles according to package instructions, then drain.
2. In a pot, heat curry paste, then add coconut milk and chicken broth.
3. Bring to a simmer, stirring in shredded chicken.
4. Serve in bowls with noodles, topped with bean sprouts and cilantro.
5. Squeeze lime juice over before serving.

Noodle Kugel

Ingredients:

- 12 oz egg noodles
- 4 eggs, beaten
- 1 cup cottage cheese
- 1 cup sour cream
- 1/2 cup sugar
- 1/4 cup butter, melted
- 1/4 cup raisins
- 1 tsp cinnamon

Instructions:

1. Preheat oven to 350°F (175°C).
2. Cook egg noodles according to package instructions, then drain.
3. In a bowl, mix eggs, cottage cheese, sour cream, sugar, butter, raisins, and cinnamon.
4. Stir in cooked noodles, then pour into a greased baking dish.
5. Bake for 45 minutes until set and golden.

Italian Pasta Salad

Ingredients:

- 12 oz rotini or penne pasta
- 1 cup cherry tomatoes, halved
- 1/2 cup black olives, sliced
- 1/2 cup mozzarella balls
- 1/4 cup red onion, chopped
- 1/4 cup olive oil
- 2 tbsp red wine vinegar
- 1 tsp Italian seasoning
- Salt and pepper to taste

Instructions:

1. Cook pasta according to package instructions, then drain and cool.
2. In a large bowl, combine pasta, tomatoes, olives, mozzarella, and onion.
3. In a small bowl, whisk together olive oil, vinegar, Italian seasoning, salt, and pepper.
4. Pour dressing over pasta and toss to combine.

Dan Dan Noodles

Ingredients:

- 8 oz wheat noodles
- 2 tbsp vegetable oil
- 1/2 lb ground pork
- 2 garlic cloves, minced
- 2 tbsp soy sauce
- 1 tbsp sesame paste
- 1 tbsp chili oil
- 1/4 cup green onions, chopped
- Crushed peanuts (for garnish)

Instructions:

1. Cook wheat noodles according to package instructions, then drain.
2. In a pan, heat oil, cook ground pork until browned.
3. Add garlic, soy sauce, sesame paste, and chili oil, cooking for 2 minutes.
4. Toss cooked noodles with the pork mixture, garnishing with green onions and peanuts before serving.

Macaroni and Cheese

Ingredients:

- 8 oz elbow macaroni
- 2 cups cheddar cheese, shredded
- 1/2 cup milk
- 1/4 cup butter
- 1/4 cup all-purpose flour
- 1/2 tsp salt
- 1/4 tsp pepper
- 1/4 tsp paprika (optional)

Instructions:

1. Cook macaroni according to package instructions, then drain.
2. In a saucepan, melt butter, stir in flour, salt, and pepper, cooking for 1 minute.
3. Gradually add milk, stirring until thickened.
4. Remove from heat, stir in cheese until melted.
5. Combine cheese sauce with macaroni, transfer to a baking dish, and bake at 350°F (175°C) for 20 minutes.

Khao Soi (Thai Coconut Curry Noodles)

Ingredients:

- 8 oz egg noodles
- 1 can coconut milk
- 2 tbsp red curry paste
- 2 cups chicken or vegetable broth
- 1 lb chicken breast, sliced
- 1 tbsp fish sauce
- Lime wedges (for serving)
- Fresh cilantro (for garnish)

Instructions:

1. Cook egg noodles according to package instructions, then drain.
2. In a pot, heat curry paste, add coconut milk and broth, simmering for 5 minutes.
3. Add chicken and fish sauce, cooking until chicken is done.
4. Serve noodles in bowls, topped with the curry sauce, and garnish with cilantro and lime.

Carbonara

Ingredients:

- 8 oz spaghetti
- 4 oz pancetta or bacon, diced
- 2 eggs
- 1/2 cup grated Parmesan cheese
- 2 garlic cloves, minced
- Salt and pepper to taste
- Fresh parsley, chopped (for garnish)

Instructions:

1. Cook spaghetti according to package instructions, then reserve 1 cup of pasta water and drain.
2. In a skillet, cook pancetta until crispy, adding garlic for the last minute.
3. In a bowl, whisk together eggs and Parmesan cheese.
4. Combine spaghetti with pancetta, then remove from heat and quickly stir in egg mixture, adding reserved pasta water as needed.
5. Season with salt and pepper, garnishing with parsley before serving.

Cold Soba Noodle Salad

Ingredients:

- 8 oz soba noodles
- 1 cup cucumber, julienned
- 1 cup carrots, julienned
- 1/4 cup scallions, chopped
- 1/4 cup soy sauce
- 2 tbsp sesame oil
- 1 tbsp rice vinegar
- Sesame seeds (for garnish)

Instructions:

1. Cook soba noodles according to package instructions, then drain and rinse with cold water.
2. In a large bowl, combine noodles, cucumber, carrots, and scallions.
3. In a small bowl, whisk together soy sauce, sesame oil, and rice vinegar.
4. Pour dressing over salad and toss to combine, garnishing with sesame seeds before serving.

Yakisoba (Japanese Stir-Fried Noodles)

Ingredients:

- 8 oz yakisoba noodles (or any stir-fried noodles)
- 1 cup sliced pork or chicken
- 1 cup cabbage, shredded
- 1 bell pepper, sliced
- 2 carrots, julienned
- 1/4 cup yakisoba sauce (or soy sauce)
- Green onions, chopped (for garnish)

Instructions:

1. Cook yakisoba noodles according to package instructions.
2. In a large skillet, stir-fry pork or chicken until cooked through.
3. Add vegetables and cook until tender.
4. Stir in cooked noodles and yakisoba sauce, mixing well.
5. Serve garnished with green onions.

Spicy Thai Noodles

Ingredients:

- 8 oz rice noodles
- 2 tbsp vegetable oil
- 1 cup shrimp or chicken
- 2 garlic cloves, minced
- 2 tbsp soy sauce
- 1 tbsp fish sauce
- 1 tbsp chili paste
- Fresh basil (for garnish)

Instructions:

1. Cook rice noodles according to package instructions, then drain.
2. Heat oil in a pan, cook shrimp or chicken until done.
3. Add garlic, soy sauce, fish sauce, and chili paste, stirring to combine.
4. Toss in cooked noodles, mixing well.
5. Serve garnished with fresh basil.

Baked Ziti

Ingredients:

- 12 oz ziti pasta
- 2 cups marinara sauce
- 1 lb ground beef or sausage
- 2 cups ricotta cheese
- 2 cups mozzarella cheese, shredded
- 1/2 cup grated Parmesan cheese
- Italian seasoning (to taste)

Instructions:

1. Preheat oven to 350°F (175°C).
2. Cook ziti according to package instructions, then drain.
3. In a skillet, brown ground meat, then stir in marinara sauce.
4. In a large bowl, combine ziti, meat sauce, ricotta, and Italian seasoning.
5. Transfer to a baking dish, top with mozzarella and Parmesan cheese, and bake for 25-30 minutes until bubbly.

Lo Mein

Ingredients:

- 8 oz lo mein noodles
- 2 tbsp vegetable oil
- 1 cup cooked chicken or beef
- 1 cup mixed vegetables (bell peppers, carrots, broccoli)
- 3 tbsp soy sauce
- 1 tbsp oyster sauce
- Green onions, chopped (for garnish)

Instructions:

1. Cook lo mein noodles according to package instructions, then drain.
2. In a large skillet, heat oil, stir-fry meat until cooked through.
3. Add mixed vegetables, cooking until tender.
4. Stir in noodles, soy sauce, and oyster sauce, tossing to combine.
5. Serve garnished with green onions.

Mie Goreng (Indonesian Fried Noodles)

Ingredients:

- 8 oz egg noodles
- 2 tbsp vegetable oil
- 2 cloves garlic, minced
- 1 onion, sliced
- 1 cup mixed vegetables (carrots, peas, bell peppers)
- 2 eggs, beaten
- 3 tbsp sweet soy sauce
- 1 tbsp soy sauce
- Green onions, sliced (for garnish)
- Fried shallots (for garnish)

Instructions:

1. Cook egg noodles according to package instructions, then drain.
2. In a large skillet, heat oil over medium heat. Add garlic and onion, cooking until fragrant.
3. Add mixed vegetables and cook until tender. Push the veggies to the side and pour in beaten eggs, scrambling until cooked.
4. Stir in the cooked noodles, sweet soy sauce, and soy sauce, mixing well.
5. Serve garnished with green onions and fried shallots.

Aglio e Olio Spaghetti

Ingredients:

- 8 oz spaghetti
- 1/2 cup olive oil
- 6 garlic cloves, sliced
- 1/2 tsp red pepper flakes
- Salt to taste
- 1/4 cup parsley, chopped
- Grated Parmesan cheese (for serving)

Instructions:

1. Cook spaghetti according to package instructions, then reserve 1 cup of pasta water and drain.
2. In a large skillet, heat olive oil over medium heat. Add garlic and red pepper flakes, sautéing until garlic is golden.
3. Add cooked spaghetti to the skillet, tossing to coat. If too dry, add reserved pasta water.
4. Season with salt and garnish with parsley and Parmesan cheese before serving.

Tantanmen (Japanese Spicy Noodles)

Ingredients:

- 8 oz ramen noodles
- 1 tbsp sesame oil
- 2 cloves garlic, minced
- 1/2 lb ground pork
- 2 tbsp tahini
- 1 tbsp soy sauce
- 1 tbsp chili oil
- 2 cups chicken broth
- Chopped green onions (for garnish)

Instructions:

1. Cook ramen noodles according to package instructions, then drain.
2. In a pot, heat sesame oil over medium heat. Add garlic and ground pork, cooking until browned.
3. Stir in tahini, soy sauce, and chili oil, mixing well.
4. Add chicken broth and bring to a simmer.
5. Serve ramen topped with the spicy broth and garnished with green onions.

Chicken Noodle Soup

Ingredients:

- 8 oz egg noodles
- 1 lb cooked chicken, shredded
- 4 cups chicken broth
- 2 carrots, sliced
- 2 celery stalks, chopped
- 1 onion, diced
- 2 cloves garlic, minced
- Salt and pepper to taste
- Fresh parsley (for garnish)

Instructions:

1. In a large pot, heat a little oil and sauté onion, garlic, carrots, and celery until softened.
2. Add chicken broth and bring to a boil.
3. Stir in egg noodles and cook according to package instructions.
4. Add shredded chicken, seasoning with salt and pepper.
5. Serve hot, garnished with fresh parsley.

Jajangmyeon (Korean Black Bean Noodles)

Ingredients:

- 8 oz wheat noodles
- 1/2 cup black bean paste (chunjang)
- 1/2 lb pork belly, diced
- 1 onion, diced
- 1 zucchini, diced
- 1 cup cabbage, shredded
- 2 tbsp vegetable oil
- 1 cup water
- Sliced cucumbers (for garnish)

Instructions:

1. Cook noodles according to package instructions, then drain.
2. In a large skillet, heat oil and sauté pork belly until browned.
3. Add onion, zucchini, and cabbage, cooking until tender.
4. Stir in black bean paste and water, simmering until thickened.
5. Serve noodles topped with the black bean sauce and garnished with sliced cucumbers.

Hakka Noodles

Ingredients:

- 8 oz hakka noodles
- 2 tbsp vegetable oil
- 1 cup mixed vegetables (bell peppers, carrots, beans)
- 2 garlic cloves, minced
- 2 tbsp soy sauce
- 1 tbsp vinegar
- 1/2 tsp black pepper
- Green onions, chopped (for garnish)

Instructions:

1. Cook hakka noodles according to package instructions, then drain.
2. In a large skillet or wok, heat oil and sauté garlic.
3. Add mixed vegetables and stir-fry until tender.
4. Stir in cooked noodles, soy sauce, vinegar, and black pepper, mixing well.
5. Serve garnished with green onions.

Bihun Goreng (Fried Rice Vermicelli)

Ingredients:

- 8 oz rice vermicelli
- 2 tbsp vegetable oil
- 2 cloves garlic, minced
- 1/2 lb shrimp or chicken, cooked
- 1 cup mixed vegetables (carrots, peas, cabbage)
- 3 tbsp soy sauce
- 1 tbsp oyster sauce
- Fresh cilantro (for garnish)

Instructions:

1. Cook rice vermicelli according to package instructions, then drain.
2. In a skillet, heat oil and sauté garlic until fragrant.
3. Add shrimp or chicken and mixed vegetables, cooking until heated through.
4. Stir in the cooked vermicelli, soy sauce, and oyster sauce, mixing well.
5. Serve garnished with fresh cilantro.

Vermicelli Salad

Ingredients:

- 8 oz rice vermicelli
- 1 cup cucumber, julienned
- 1 cup carrots, julienned
- 1/2 cup fresh herbs (mint, cilantro, basil)
- 1/4 cup lime juice
- 2 tbsp fish sauce
- 1 tbsp sugar
- Crushed peanuts (for garnish)

Instructions:

1. Cook rice vermicelli according to package instructions, then drain and cool.
2. In a large bowl, combine vermicelli, cucumber, carrots, and fresh herbs.
3. In a small bowl, whisk together lime juice, fish sauce, and sugar.
4. Pour dressing over salad and toss to combine.
5. Serve garnished with crushed peanuts.

Noodles with Garlic and Oil

Ingredients:

- 8 oz spaghetti or linguine
- 1/4 cup olive oil
- 4 cloves garlic, thinly sliced
- 1/2 tsp red pepper flakes
- Salt to taste
- Fresh parsley, chopped (for garnish)
- Grated Parmesan cheese (optional)

Instructions:

1. Cook the pasta according to package instructions until al dente. Drain and set aside.
2. In a large skillet, heat olive oil over medium heat. Add garlic and red pepper flakes, cooking until garlic is golden.
3. Add the cooked noodles to the skillet and toss to coat in the garlic oil. Season with salt.
4. Serve garnished with fresh parsley and Parmesan cheese if desired.

Beef Stroganoff Noodles

Ingredients:

- 8 oz egg noodles
- 1 lb beef sirloin, thinly sliced
- 1 onion, chopped
- 2 cups mushrooms, sliced
- 2 cups beef broth
- 1 cup sour cream
- 2 tbsp flour
- 2 tbsp butter
- Salt and pepper to taste
- Fresh parsley, chopped (for garnish)

Instructions:

1. Cook egg noodles according to package instructions; drain and set aside.
2. In a large skillet, melt butter over medium heat. Add onions and mushrooms, sautéing until tender.
3. Add beef slices and cook until browned. Sprinkle flour over the mixture, stirring to combine.
4. Gradually add beef broth, stirring until the mixture thickens. Reduce heat and stir in sour cream.
5. Serve over egg noodles, garnished with fresh parsley.

Thai Peanut Noodles

Ingredients:

- 8 oz rice noodles
- 1/2 cup peanut butter
- 1/4 cup soy sauce
- 2 tbsp lime juice
- 1 tbsp brown sugar
- 2 cloves garlic, minced
- 1 cup shredded carrots
- 1 red bell pepper, sliced
- Chopped peanuts and cilantro (for garnish)

Instructions:

1. Cook rice noodles according to package instructions; drain and set aside.
2. In a bowl, whisk together peanut butter, soy sauce, lime juice, brown sugar, and garlic until smooth.
3. In a large bowl, combine cooked noodles, shredded carrots, and bell pepper.
4. Pour the peanut sauce over the noodles and toss to combine.
5. Serve garnished with chopped peanuts and cilantro.

Italian Gnocchi

Ingredients:

- 2 cups potato gnocchi
- 1/4 cup olive oil
- 2 cloves garlic, minced
- 1 cup cherry tomatoes, halved
- 1/4 cup fresh basil, chopped
- Salt and pepper to taste
- Grated Parmesan cheese (for serving)

Instructions:

1. Cook gnocchi according to package instructions; drain and set aside.
2. In a skillet, heat olive oil over medium heat. Add garlic and cook until fragrant.
3. Add cherry tomatoes and cook until they begin to soften.
4. Add cooked gnocchi to the skillet, tossing to coat. Season with salt, pepper, and fresh basil.
5. Serve topped with grated Parmesan cheese.

Shanghai Noodles with Pork

Ingredients:

- 8 oz Shanghai noodles
- 1/2 lb ground pork
- 2 tbsp soy sauce
- 1 tbsp oyster sauce
- 1 cup bok choy, chopped
- 1 carrot, julienned
- 2 cloves garlic, minced
- 2 tbsp vegetable oil

Instructions:

1. Cook Shanghai noodles according to package instructions; drain and set aside.
2. In a large skillet, heat vegetable oil over medium heat. Add ground pork and cook until browned.
3. Add garlic, bok choy, and carrot, stirring until vegetables are tender.
4. Stir in cooked noodles, soy sauce, and oyster sauce, mixing well.
5. Serve hot.

Shrimp Scampi Pasta

Ingredients:

- 8 oz linguine
- 1 lb shrimp, peeled and deveined
- 1/4 cup olive oil
- 4 cloves garlic, minced
- 1/2 tsp red pepper flakes
- 1/2 cup white wine
- 1/4 cup lemon juice
- 1/4 cup fresh parsley, chopped
- Salt and pepper to taste

Instructions:

1. Cook linguine according to package instructions; drain and set aside.
2. In a large skillet, heat olive oil over medium heat. Add garlic and red pepper flakes, cooking until fragrant.
3. Add shrimp and cook until pink. Pour in white wine and lemon juice, simmering for a few minutes.
4. Toss in the cooked linguine and fresh parsley. Season with salt and pepper before serving.

Miso Ramen

Ingredients:

- 4 oz ramen noodles
- 2 cups chicken or vegetable broth
- 2 tbsp miso paste
- 1 cup bok choy, chopped
- 1/2 cup sliced mushrooms
- 2 green onions, sliced
- Soft-boiled egg (for topping)

Instructions:

1. Cook ramen noodles according to package instructions; drain and set aside.
2. In a pot, heat the broth and stir in miso paste until dissolved.
3. Add bok choy and mushrooms, simmering until tender.
4. Serve ramen topped with the broth, green onions, and a soft-boiled egg.

Khichdi (Indian Rice and Noodle Dish)

Ingredients:

- 1/2 cup rice
- 1/2 cup noodles
- 1/2 cup split yellow lentils (moong dal)
- 1 onion, chopped
- 2 carrots, diced
- 1 tsp turmeric powder
- 4 cups water
- Salt to taste
- Ghee or oil for cooking

Instructions:

1. In a pot, heat ghee or oil and sauté onions until golden.
2. Add carrots, rice, lentils, noodles, turmeric, and water.
3. Season with salt and bring to a boil. Reduce heat and simmer until everything is cooked through.
4. Serve hot.

Noodle Salad with Vegetables

Ingredients:

- 8 oz pasta (e.g., soba, rice noodles)
- 1 cup cucumber, julienned
- 1 bell pepper, sliced
- 1 carrot, grated
- 1/4 cup green onions, sliced
- 1/4 cup cilantro, chopped
- 1/4 cup soy sauce
- 2 tbsp sesame oil
- 1 tbsp rice vinegar
- 1 tsp sesame seeds

Instructions:

1. Cook the pasta according to package instructions; drain and rinse under cold water.
2. In a large bowl, combine the cooked noodles with cucumber, bell pepper, carrot, green onions, and cilantro.
3. In a small bowl, whisk together soy sauce, sesame oil, rice vinegar, and sesame seeds.
4. Pour the dressing over the noodle salad and toss to combine. Serve chilled or at room temperature.

Hungarian Noodles with Cabbage

Ingredients:

- 8 oz egg noodles
- 1/2 head cabbage, shredded
- 1 onion, chopped
- 2 tbsp butter
- 1 tsp paprika
- Salt and pepper to taste

Instructions:

1. Cook the egg noodles according to package instructions; drain and set aside.
2. In a large skillet, melt butter over medium heat. Add onions and cook until translucent.
3. Stir in cabbage and cook until softened. Add paprika, salt, and pepper.
4. Toss the cooked noodles with the cabbage mixture. Serve warm.

Zucchini Noodles with Marinara

Ingredients:

- 4 medium zucchinis, spiralized
- 2 cups marinara sauce
- 2 cloves garlic, minced
- 1 tbsp olive oil
- Salt and pepper to taste
- Fresh basil (for garnish)

Instructions:

1. In a skillet, heat olive oil over medium heat. Add garlic and sauté until fragrant.
2. Add marinara sauce and bring to a simmer.
3. Stir in spiralized zucchini noodles and cook for 2-3 minutes until tender.
4. Season with salt and pepper, and serve garnished with fresh basil.

Curry Noodles

Ingredients:

- 8 oz noodles (e.g., rice or udon)
- 1 cup coconut milk
- 2 tbsp curry paste
- 1 cup mixed vegetables (carrots, bell peppers, peas)
- 2 tbsp soy sauce
- Fresh cilantro (for garnish)

Instructions:

1. Cook the noodles according to package instructions; drain and set aside.
2. In a pot, heat coconut milk and curry paste over medium heat. Stir until well combined.
3. Add mixed vegetables and simmer until tender.
4. Toss in the cooked noodles and soy sauce. Serve garnished with fresh cilantro.

Fideo (Spanish Noodle Dish)

Ingredients:

- 8 oz fideo noodles
- 2 cups chicken or vegetable broth
- 1 onion, chopped
- 1 bell pepper, diced
- 2 cloves garlic, minced
- 1 tsp smoked paprika
- Salt and pepper to taste

Instructions:

1. In a large skillet, heat oil over medium heat. Add onions, bell pepper, and garlic, sautéing until softened.
2. Add fideo noodles and cook until lightly toasted.
3. Pour in broth, smoked paprika, salt, and pepper; bring to a boil.
4. Reduce heat and simmer until noodles are cooked and liquid is absorbed. Serve warm.

Spicy Sichuan Noodles

Ingredients:

- 8 oz noodles (e.g., egg or wheat)
- 2 tbsp Sichuan peppercorns
- 2 tbsp chili oil
- 2 cloves garlic, minced
- 2 tbsp soy sauce
- 1 tbsp rice vinegar
- Green onions and sesame seeds (for garnish)

Instructions:

1. Cook the noodles according to package instructions; drain and set aside.
2. In a pan, heat chili oil and add Sichuan peppercorns, cooking until fragrant.
3. Stir in garlic, soy sauce, and rice vinegar.
4. Toss the cooked noodles in the sauce and serve garnished with green onions and sesame seeds.

Noodle Bowl with Tofu and Veggies

Ingredients:

- 8 oz noodles (e.g., soba or rice)
- 1 block firm tofu, cubed
- 1 cup mixed vegetables (broccoli, bell pepper, carrots)
- 2 tbsp soy sauce
- 1 tbsp sesame oil
- 1 tsp ginger, grated
- Green onions (for garnish)

Instructions:

1. Cook noodles according to package instructions; drain and set aside.
2. In a skillet, heat sesame oil and sauté tofu until golden. Add mixed vegetables and cook until tender.
3. Stir in soy sauce and ginger, mixing well.
4. Serve the tofu and veggies over the noodles, garnished with green onions.

Bun Rieu (Vietnamese Crab Noodle Soup)

Ingredients:

- 8 oz rice vermicelli noodles
- 1 lb crab meat
- 6 cups chicken or seafood broth
- 2 tomatoes, chopped
- 1/4 cup fish sauce
- 2 green onions, sliced
- Fresh herbs (basil, cilantro) for garnish

Instructions:

1. Cook the rice vermicelli noodles according to package instructions; drain and set aside.
2. In a pot, bring the broth to a boil. Add tomatoes and fish sauce, simmering for 10 minutes.
3. Stir in crab meat and cook until heated through.
4. Serve noodles in bowls, ladle the broth and crab mixture over, and garnish with green onions and fresh herbs.

Soba Noodles with Dipping Sauce

Ingredients:

- 8 oz soba noodles
- 1/4 cup soy sauce
- 2 tbsp mirin
- 1 tbsp rice vinegar
- 1 tsp sesame oil
- Green onions, sliced (for garnish)
- Wasabi (optional)

Instructions:

1. Cook the soba noodles according to package instructions; drain and rinse under cold water.
2. In a small bowl, mix soy sauce, mirin, rice vinegar, and sesame oil to make the dipping sauce.
3. Serve the soba noodles chilled or at room temperature, alongside the dipping sauce and garnished with sliced green onions and wasabi if desired.

Pancit (Filipino Stir-Fried Noodles)

Ingredients:

- 8 oz rice noodles (or any stir-fried noodle)
- 2 tbsp vegetable oil
- 1 onion, sliced
- 2 cloves garlic, minced
- 1 cup carrots, julienned
- 1 cup green beans, cut into 1-inch pieces
- 1 bell pepper, sliced
- 3 tbsp soy sauce
- 2 tbsp oyster sauce
- Salt and pepper to taste
- Green onions and lemon wedges (for garnish)

Instructions:

1. Cook the rice noodles according to package instructions; drain and set aside.
2. In a large skillet or wok, heat vegetable oil over medium heat. Add onions and garlic, sautéing until fragrant.
3. Add carrots, green beans, and bell pepper; stir-fry until vegetables are tender.
4. Toss in the cooked noodles, soy sauce, and oyster sauce, stirring well to combine. Season with salt and pepper.
5. Serve hot, garnished with green onions and lemon wedges.

www.ingramcontent.com/pod-product-compliance
Lightning Source LLC
LaVergne TN
LVHW081338060526
838201LV00055B/2714